OWL TV

book of ANIMALS

Megan Lander & Dave Rogers

Contents

Headway · Hodder & Stoughton

Photography by Megan Lander

Introduction

Do you know what a numbat is? Did you know that porcupine quills are often used as fishing floats? Well, I certainly didn't before I started presenting OWL TV!

Since our first series, we have filmed an amazing variety of animals and conservation projects in countries around the world including Australia, the Seychelles, Kenya, Madagascar, Morocco, Gibraltar, Canada, America, Belize, Costa Rica and, of course, Great Britain!

So, we thought it might be a good idea to feature some of the animals which have appeared in the series in a book – and here it is – the *OWL TV Book of Animals*!

It has now become more important than ever for us to protect our planet and the incredible variety of animals that share it with us, because many of them are in danger of becoming extinct.

Each year, thousands of dolphins and seals are killed by fishermen; hundreds of elephants are shot for their ivory tusks and black rhinos for their horns. Each minute forty hectares of valuable tropical rain forest are destroyed, contributing to the frightening figure of one thousand animals and plants which become extinct every year.

Many animals are used for unnecessary laboratory experiments, others are killed for their fur and thousands are taken from their natural habitat to supply the world's pet trade. And, if that isn't enough, we continue to dump thousands of tonnes of oil and other chemicals into our seas and rivers and we pollute the atmosphere to such an extent that the hole in the ozone layer is now the size of the United States!

It may all sound depressing and hopeless, but it's not too late and each one of us can play an important part in helping protect the world we live in.

At the back of the book is a list of names and addresses of conservation organisations you can either join or write to for information. They all need your help and are looking forward to hearing from you.

Good luck and I hope you enjoy reading about some of the animals we have met whilst making OWL TV!

Love

HOME	STATUS
Gibraltar, Algeria, Morocco	Many become endangered due to loss of habitat in Algeria and overfeeding in Gibraltar
DIET	
Fruit, leaves, bark, roots	
	YOUNG
	One baby at a time

Barbary Ape

Gibraltar's primate soldiers

Although called apes, Barbary Apes are actually a species of monkey with virtually no tail. They are survivors of a long line of North African Macaque monkeys and are the only members of this tail-less tribe living wild in Europe.

Barbary Apes became protected by the British Army following the Great Siege of 1779–1783 when the Spaniards tried to surprise the British by climbing the steep eastern rock. They woke the apes who screeched a loud warning, alerting the defending troops.

During the First World War, hungry apes raided the town in search of food and became such pests that the army decided to feed them on a regular basis to stop them terrorising the local population. In 1915, the British Army created a new post for an 'Officer in charge of the Apes'.

The apes have now become a tourist attraction but their visitors cannot resist feeding the animals with chocolate, sweets and popcorn. This has caused major dietary problems. The apes have become more and more unhealthy and overweight and, together with their lack of privacy, it has meant that many have stopped breeding and are reaching only half their normal life expectancy of 25 years.

The Tourism Agency has decided to make a special nature reserve for the apes where they will have a properly controlled diet and more suitable surroundings. It will be run by conservationalists who will work alongside the Army's 'Officer in charge of the Apes'. It is hoped that 250,000 tourists will visit the reserve each year, paying a small entrance fee, and that this income will help to give the Barbary Apes a new lease of life.

HOME	YOUNG
Coastal areas from India to Australia	Approximately 30 eggs are laid at a time. (Baby crocodiles have a special 'egg tooth' or snout for breaking through shell.)
DIET	
Fish, small and large mammals	
STATUS	
Not endangered	

Estuarine crocodile

The ancient reptilian man-eater

left: a Freshwater crocodile; **above:** an Estuarine crocodile; **right:** a crocodile's scutes.

The Estuarine, or Saltwater, crocodile is the world's largest living reptile and the most dangerous. It lives mainly in and around coastal areas, estuaries and swamps, from India to Northern Australia. These crocodiles have been known to swim out to sea and sometimes travel hundreds of kilometres, from one coast to another.

Estuarine crocodiles can grow up to more than 6 m in length and, although it is not known why this species is so aggressive, they kill many hundreds of people each year. Submerged in the water, with only its eyes and nostrils showing, an Estuarine crocodile can suddenly launch itself at its unsuspecting prey. Large animals are dragged into the water and drowned or killed by the crocodile as it twists and rolls over.

It is well-equipped for a predatory life. Its jaws are large and strong with powerful teeth and the scales, or scutes, on its back disperse the water, helping it to move without creating a sound or a ripple.

The Estuarine crocodile sometimes lives in the same waters as the Freshwater crocodile, which is harmless to Man and only eats fish and small aquatic animals. They say that you can safely swim in the same pool as a Freshwater crocodile, but you have to make quite sure that you know the difference between the two!

Dolphin

HOME	STATUS
Many coastal and river areas around world	Exact numbers not known, but some species endangered
DIET	**YOUNG**
Fish	One calf at a time, weaned after five months or more

The mammal which lost its feet

More than 50 million years ago, dolphins and whales were land animals with hooves and probably lived in coastal areas where they caught fish by wading into shallow waters. They eventually took to the sea and became marine mammals, their feet slowly shrinking and their tails turning into flukes. Their pectoral, or front, fins are now all that remains of their feet.

Dolphins are found in many parts of the world and are considered to be the most intelligent and friendly of the marine animals. However, it is unusual for them to be quite as friendly as they are at Monkey Mia in Western Australia. Almost every day, a family of up to seventeen wild Bottle-Nose dolphins swims into the shallow water at the edge of the beach to meet the people gathered there. They enjoy cruising up and down the beach, observing the people with their bright, beady eyes and even taking fish from their hands.

A Bottle-Nose dolphin comes for lunch at Monkey Mia.

Sadly, thousands of dolphins are killed every year by swimming into tuna fish drift nets. Walls of these nets, which can be up to 50 km long, are laid across the sea and catch not

only tuna, but anything else, including dolphins, unlucky enough to swim into them. If all the nets put out in the North Pacific for just one night were laid end to end, they would go round the earth twice!

Another method of fishing for tuna is by the traditional 'pole and line' with which the tuna are caught one at a time. If you buy tuna fish at your grocery shop or supermarket, look out for tins marked 'dolphin friendly'.

Dolphins' fins are as different from each other as people's faces are.

Elephant

HOME	STATUS
Africa and Asia	700,000 left in Africa
DIET	**YOUNG**
Trees, grass, leaves, fruit	One calf at a time; twins on rare occasions

The giant tusked mammal that 'purrs'

There are two species of elephant, the African and the Indian, or Asian. The African is the larger of the two and can measure up to 3.6 m in height and weigh up to 6,000 kg. African elephants also have bigger ears, longer tusks and two 'lips' at the end of their trunks, whereas the Asian has just one.

While the Indian elephant lives in shady forest areas, the African often inhabits dry, open plains and cannot easily find shelter from the strong midday sun. However, it gets around this problem by flapping its large fan-like ears in order to keep its body cool.

Both species can sleep standing or lying on one side. An elephant will sometimes gather a pile of vegetation together and then rest its head on it, like a pillow. Their diet is entirely vegetarian and includes grass, foliage and fruit. Their trunks are used to gather the food and then transfer it into their mouths. Their tusks are used mainly for tearing bark from trees and digging holes in the ground to look for water during times of drought.

We all know the 'trumpeting' sounds elephants make, but it is less well known that elephants also 'purr'! Their low, tummy-rumbling noise will stop if someone approaches and the sudden silence alerts the rest of the herd, which also becomes silent. Only when the danger has passed does the 'purring' start again and then the herd knows that all is well.

These two young African elephants, rescued from a culling in Zambia, can now enjoy their mud bath in safety.

IN DANGER!

Although there is now a ban on the trade of ivory, elephants have become an endangered species because they are killed for their valuable ivory tusks, which are carved to make ornaments and jewellery. There were probably 10 million elephants roaming Africa 500 years ago but, in 1969, there were only 2 million and now there are less than 600,000. Even with special reserves and armed guard protection, over 50,000 elephants have been killed every year. For every elephant shot by poachers, 3 others, usually calves who depend on their mothers, will also die.

Giraffe

HOME	STATUS
Africa	Used to live in many African countries, but thousands of giraffes have been killed for their hides
DIET	
Leaves	
YOUNG	
A single calf which can walk within an hour of birth	

The tallest animal on earth

There are thought to be nine different species of giraffe in the world. Each one is identified by height, colour patterns and the number of horns, of which there can be up to five. The tallest species is the Masai.

The giraffe is the tallest living land animal and towers up to 5.5 m above the ground. Even though it has such a long neck, the giraffe has the same number of vertebrae in its spine as a man and manages to support it with incredibly strong muscles.

Although this long neck is useful for reaching leaves on high trees, the giraffe cannot reach the ground to drink or eat without spreading its legs wide enough apart to be able to lower its shoulders. The giraffe's blood supply system has been specially designed by nature to prevent a sudden rush of blood to its head when it bends down to drink.

The giraffe has a prehensile tongue, 50 cm long, which it uses to pluck leaves neatly from branches, thus avoiding the thorns. Because the tongue spends so much time out of the giraffe's mouth, it is often coloured grey or black in order to reduce the risk of sunburn.

Although awkwardly proportioned, giraffes are surprisingly graceful. They can run faster than a horse at speeds of up to 29 mph (46 kmph) across the open African savanna, with their necks swaying gently from side to side.

ROONEY LEGEND!

Their height and good eyesight allow them to see enemies approaching from a distance and they probably have the greatest range of vision of any mammal. They have very few predators although a lion may take a young calf and several lions sometimes gang together to attack an adult. However, attackers should be wary, because the giraffe's long legs can kill a lion with one blow.

Kangaroo

HOME	STATUS
Australia and New Guinea	Most species not endangered
DIET	**YOUNG**
Mainly grass	One baby born per year

Australia's unwanted jumpers

The fifty-five different species of kangaroo, wallaby and wallaroo make up the family Macropodidae (from *macropus* meaning 'big foot').

Kangaroos are probably the best-known of the Australian marsupials, or pouched animals, although they are regarded as pests by farmers. Hundreds of thousands of miles

going...

of fencing have been erected around sheep grazing pastures to stop kangaroos from eating the grass. However, because they are such good jumpers (they have been known to leap over fences 2.7 m high) and are particlarly good at squeezing through badly-repaired fences, farmers often resort to shooting them. In a single year, on just 9 sheep farms, 140,000 kangaroos were killed.

When a baby kangaroo is born, it is only 19 mm long. As soon as it emerges, it drags itself up into the mother's pouch and latches straight on to one of her four teats. It will then stay in the pouch for 8 months, by which time it will weigh nearly 4.5 kg. It continues to be suckled for up to 6 months after it has left the pouch and if the young kangaroo, or 'joey', gets thirsty, it can just put its head back into the pouch in order to get a drink. If there are any signs of danger, the joey will leap into the safety of the pouch where it will stay until its mother gives the all-clear.

15

HOME	STATUS
Australia	Exact numbers not known
DIET	**YOUNG**
Eucalyptus leaves	Usually one baby is born at a time

Koala

One of the world's fussiest eaters

Although popularly known as a bear, the koala is actually a marsupial, or pouched, animal.

Koalas spend as many as twenty hours a day dozing or sleeping, usually curled up in a tree fork, high above the ground. They are excellent climbers, grasping on to tree trunks and branches with their sharp claws. Only occasionally do they come down to the ground in order to shuffle across to the next tree, which may have been too far away to jump to.

Koalas are very fussy about their diet and will only eat about 20 of the 350 different species of eucalyptus or 'gum tree' leaves.

Baby koalas are born in the spring or summer and are no bigger than a grape. Soon after birth, the young animal climbs blindly into the protection of its mother's pouch where it stays for about six months, feeding on her milk. After this time it leaves the pouch, but still travels with the mother, clinging on to her back, where it will remain until the next spring when it is old enough to venture out on its own.

IN DANGER!

Large numbers of koalas have been killed over the years for their thick, warm fur. Today, they are protected by law, but are still threatened as many thousands of acres of their home, the eucalyptus forests, are being chopped down to make way for farmland and housing developments. In some areas, where koalas have been left stranded in small patches of forest, local councils have been planting avenues of trees to link up all the isolated areas.

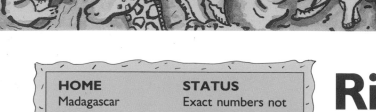

HOME	STATUS
Madagascar	Exact numbers not known
DIET	**YOUNG**
Vegetarian	One or two babies

Ring-tailed lemur

The ghosts of Madagascar

Lemurs – the name means 'ghosts' – are found only on the island of Madagascar. Madagascar is the fifth largest island in the world and has been separated from the south-east coast of Africa for about 60 million years. It has one of the most unusual groups of wildlife anywhere on earth.

Lemurs are the best-known of all Madagascar's animals. There are about twenty species, some of which have been discovered only recently. They range in size from one as small as a mouse to another as large as a chimpanzee. They are easily distinguished from true monkeys by their fox-like muzzles and their very large eyes.

A Ring-tailed lemur measures about 1.2 m from its head to the end of its dramatically-striped tail. Unlike most lemurs, which inhabit thick forests, the ring-tailed species lives in thinly-wooded, dry and rocky country, foraging for its vegetarian diet of shoots and leaves. They seem to be less at home in the trees than other lemurs and make sure that, when they do leave the ground, they travel along the larger, more steady branches.

Whilst most lemurs are nocturnal, the Ring-tailed lemur is diurnal, or active during the day. When it meets an enemy, it will raise its scent-smeared tail high in the air and point it in the direction of its rival.

Lemurs love sunbathing and can sometimes be seen sitting with their open arms resting elegantly on their knees.

IN DANGER!
All lemurs and much of Madagascar's other wildlife are threatened by the continuing destruction of the forests for fuel, timber and farmland. In some areas, the loss of trees has led to such severe soil erosion that water around the coast has been dyed a deep red by the soil washed into it.

HOME	STATUS
Africa and Gir forest in India	Endangered in India
DIET	YOUNG
Meat and sometimes fruit	One to five at a time. Lion cubs are born blind with spotted coats

Lion

The big cat with a fear of porcupines

Lions, known as the 'King of the Beasts', are members of the cat family and roam the open plains of Africa.

Lions can run at speeds of up to 40 mph (64 kmph) but only in short bursts, and they can make running leaps of up to 12 m. Although males will not normally climb trees, lionesses may jump up on to low branches to sunbathe.

They live in open country in groups of up to twenty, known as prides, which are made up of one or more mature male lions and a number of lionesses with their cubs. When hunting, they work as a team, stalking and then ambushing their prey. Although the

lionesses often make the kill, the lions eat first, hence the expression 'eating the lion's share'. The lionesses eat next, followed by the cubs. Their main food is antelope and zebra although, when very hungry, they will eat almost anything from rats to giraffe and even porcupines.

Lions hunt at night, avoiding the light and heat of the day and stalk their prey in silence. In the early hours of the morning, a lion's roar can be heard over some distance and often continues all day. Sometimes others will join in and as many as ten lions can be heard roaring together across the African plains.

Although they have no natural enemies other than Man, lions, especially young, inexperienced cubs, may be kicked by a zebra or impaled on the horns of an antelope. A would-be porcupine eater can easily come off worst as a porcupine will run backwards and stick its sharp, pointed quills into the oncoming predator.

IN DANGER!
Lions were once common throughout southern Europe, southern Asia and Africa. The last lion in Europe died between AD 80 and 100 and the only lions left in Asia now are in the Gir Forest in north-west India, where there are probably as few as 300.

HOME	STATUS
Central and South America	Exact numbers not known
DIET	**YOUNG**
Fruit and insects	One baby is born per year

Squirrel monkey

The brainy South American primate

The Squirrel monkey is one of the most widely-found monkeys in Central and South America and is considered one of the most charming and beautiful. It is most remarkable for its large skull. Relative to the size of its body, its brain is bigger than Man's! It has a long tail which is slightly prehensile, which means it can be used as an extra hand. This makes the Squirrel monkey very good at climbing.

Squirrel monkeys live in large groups and travel across the scrub woodlands in search of lizards and eggs, although their favourite food is insects. They spend most of their time foraging, or looking for food. When they have eaten all the food in one area, the group moves off to another one.

Unlike some species of monkey, Squirrel monkeys are very friendly towards each other and do not usually fight to protect their territory.

IN DANGER!
Although there is still a large number of Squirrel monkeys left in the wild, they are used for medical experiments both in Britain and overseas and large colonies are kept in laboratories for this purpose.

Squirrel monkeys have very sharp, narrow teeth which help them eat quickly.

Woolly monkey

HOME	STATUS
South America	Could soon become endangered
DIET	**YOUNG**
Fruit, seeds, leaves, flowers	One baby born at a time

The edible treetop primates

Their diet is extremely varied, consisting of fruit, seeds, leaves, shoots, flowers and the occasional insect. Many of the fruits which they like to eat have large seeds but only a little flesh, so they swallow the whole fruit to save time. The seeds then pass through their digestive system and are later left in droppings some distance from the original tree. When they germinate, the seeds provide more trees and help to ensure the survival of the rain forest.

Woolly monkeys live high up in the canopy of the Amazonian rain forests of South America, sometimes as much as 60 m above the ground. Because the branches and foliage are so dense, the monkeys find it difficult to see each other and they give loud calls to keep in touch.

The monkeys spend most of their time travelling in groups through the treetops, feeding, resting and sometimes basking in the sun on the branches of giant trees which emerge from the top of the canopy.

IN DANGER!
The woolly monkey is one of the most threatened South American primates. Even though, for thousands of years, the forest Indians have hunted and eaten the monkeys without affecting their numbers, the destruction of their rain forest home for farming, timber and other industrial developments is now seriously endangering their survival.

HOME	STATUS
South West Australia	Approximately 2,000 left
DIET	**YOUNG**
Termites	Four at a time

Numbat

The marsupial with a taste for termites

Numbats live in South Western Australia and are so rare that even most Australians have never heard of them! Although numbats are marsupials, they do not have a pouch. Their young simply have to hang on to the mother's teats and hope for the best, partially protected by the long hair on her stomach.

Numbats are also the only marsupial to exist entirely on termites – a type of white ant. In fact, numbats eat up to 20,000 termites every day, which is equal to a tenth of their entire body weight!

The white bands across the numbat's back act as a form of camouflage and help break up its shape against a background of logs and twigs. It often stands up on its hind legs to watch out for predators and, if it sees one, will scamper quickly into a small hollow log to hide from the enemy.

Their main predators are foxes, which were introduced to Australia for hunting by European settlers. The fox population has now reached such a level that numbats and many of Australia's other small mammals are being killed by these foreign carnivores.

IN DANGER!

As with the habitat of so many other animals, the wooded areas where numbats used to live have been cleared for farming. So much of their natural habitat has now gone that there are thought to be only 2,000 of them still living in the wild.

As there are now so few left, a special captive breeding programme has been set up at Western Australia's Perth Zoo and groups of numbats born there are being released into the wild to help build up their numbers.

Snowy owl

The Arctic lemming hunter

The beautiful Snowy owl generally lives in the frozen Arctic but sometimes flies south to spend the winter in Scandinavia, Canada, the USA and Russia. Its feathers are pure white with dark, barred markings, which act as a perfect camouflage in its snow-covered surroundings.

It has a wingspan of 1.6 m and glides silently over the northern tundra (a barren region where the ground is almost always frozen and only mosses and small shrubs can grow) in search of its favourite food – lemmings and voles. It is one of the world's most powerful owls and can carry off large numbers of lemmings at a time. It also catches fish and lies in wait by the banks of rivers and lakes,

suddenly plunging its claws into the water to grab its prey.

The Snowy owl's food supply changes from year to year and sometimes there may be very few voles and lemmings to be found. When this happens, the female owl, which in good years may lay up to fourteen eggs, will lay only one or two or may not bother to nest at all. In this way, she can always be sure that her chicks will have enough to eat.

HOME	STATUS
Africa and Arabia	Not considered to be endangered
DIET	YOUNG
Omnivorous, but mainly vegetarian	Six to eight eggs are laid at a time

Ostrich

The fearless, two-legged rubbish bin

Ostriches, the world's largest living birds, live in most areas of Africa and are reputed to be very dangerous, particularly during the breeding season. Their huge, powerfully-clawed legs can give a fatal kick. Ostriches also appear to be totally fearless, and there is one story of an Ostrich rushing on to a railway track to do battle with an oncoming train.

The Ostrich cannot fly but can run at speeds of up to 45 mph (72 kmph). Car drivers have sometimes seen an Ostrich running neck and neck alongside them!

The Ostrich is an omnivore, which means that it eats both plants and animals. Its usual diet consists of grass, seeds, insects and very small animals, but its amazingly elastic throat can manage objects the size of a grapefruit. Records show that one male bird swallowed a 90 cm long piece of rope, a roll of film, an alarm clock key, a bicycle valve, a pencil, a comb, three gloves, a handkerchief, pieces of a gold necklace and two collar studs. Not surprisingly, he did not eat another meal!

You have probably heard that an Ostrich buries its head in the sand when it is frightened. In fact, what happens is that, while sitting on its nest, the Ostrich lays its head and neck flat along the ground, giving any predator a view of what appears to be nothing more than a mound of earth.

HOME	STATUS
Sichuan, Garvsu and Shaanxi provinces of China	Endangered – only 1,000 are left in the wild
DIET	**YOUNG**
Bamboo	One, two, or even three babies are born at a time, but only one will survive

Giant panda

The world's largest racoon?

Although it is sometimes called a bear, the Giant panda is thought by some scientists to be a member of the much smaller racoon family.

Pandas live in the Sichuan, Garvsu and Shaanxi provinces of China, and live on a diet of bamboo shoots and roots. In order to fill their large bodies (1.5 m long) they have to spend between ten and twelve hours each day eating. Pandas do not often have to drink water, especially in the spring when up to ninety per cent of bamboo shoots are made up of water.

Pandas' sharp claws make it possible for them to climb trees in order to escape from predators, but they are not so good at climbing down again. Sometimes they get stuck and decide to come down head first – with unfortunate results!

Pandas have very strong jaws and teeth to crush the tough stems of the bamboo.

IN DANGER!

A break in the supply of bamboo shoots can be disastrous for pandas. The Bamboo has an unusual life cycle, and every 40 to 120 years, depending on the species, the plants bloom, drop their seeds and die. At one time, the pandas would have just moved on to another bamboo forest to feed, but, since China has had such a massive increase in its population, huge areas of land have been taken over for farming and there are very few places left for the pandas to go.

There are now only 1,000 pandas left in the wild. A number of pandas have been taken to zoos around the world to help build up their numbers, but they do not seem to breed well in captivity.

HOME
Australia

YOUNG
One to four white
eggs are laid

DIET
Fish and crustaceans

Australian pelican

The bird with the built-in fishing net

Pelicans have lived in Australia for a long time. Their fossil remains have been found in layers of soil dating back 30 or 40 million years. The prehistoric pelicans were very similar to the present day ones, but probably had shorter legs and were slightly smaller.

The upper part of a pelican's beak is flattened and the lower part carries a pouch that can stretch to an enormous size. It can hold 17 pints of water and is used as a dip net for catching and storing fish.

Pelicans are very sociable and nest in large colonies of up to 1,000 birds. They breed on isolated islands and build nests on the ground, although they do sometimes nest in low trees. The babies are born naked and blind, but quickly grow a soft down. Both parents feed the young, at first dribbling regurgitated food out of the end of their beaks and into the chicks' mouths, but, after a few days, the chicks are strong enough to stick their heads into their parents' pouches to eat the fish whole.

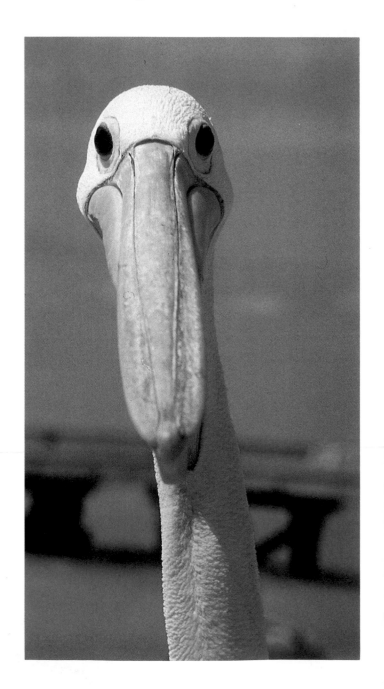

Pelicans fly in a loose V-formation or in line when in groups. Their wings are flapped leisurely several times and then spread flat in long glides that can carry the birds in soaring circles as high as 3,000 m. During droughts, some have reached Indonesia, the Solomon Islands and New Zealand.

Pelicans are long-living birds and, although the accepted record is 52 years, the Emperor Maximilian is said to have had a pelican which lived for more than 80 years!

A pelican has a long neck but a stocky body and short legs which account for its waddling gait!

HOME	STATUS
The Arctic	Only 25,000 left
DIET	**YOUNG**
Carnivorous – seals, whales, birds, eggs and small mammals	One to three cubs are born at a time

Polar bear

The Arctic carnivore with webbed feet

The Polar bear is one of the world's largest carnivores and, although it lives in the frozen Arctic, it is perfectly adapted to life in this hostile environment.

It has a thick winter coat and a layer of fat which protect it from the cold air and water. Apart from its nose and foot pads it is completly covered in hair and its short ears also help reduce the loss of heat from its body. The mother's milk has a particularly high fat content, which helps her cubs grow strong quickly during the first four months of their life before they leave the protection of the snow den where they are born.

As Polar bears live on the sea ice, they move south during the winter when the sea freezes over and then return back north again when it melts in the summer. They may travel 43 miles (69 km) or more in a day and are equipped with a waterproof coat and partially-webbed feet which enable them to swim long distances between one ice floe and another.

The Polar bear's main source of food is the Ringed and Bearded seal, which it catches beside open water or at breathing holes in the ice. Although the Polar bear usually lives and hunts alone, groups of up to 40 bears will come together to feed off the dead bodies of whales or walruses. When their normal food is in short supply, they may eat small mammals, birds, eggs and plants and can sometimes be seen raiding the dustbins and rubbish tips of Arctic towns and villages.

IN DANGER!
Today, there are only 25,000 Polar bears in the world. Although they are protected from hunting by international agreement, Eskimos, Inuits and other subsistence farmers in the Arctic are still allowed to kill them for food.

HOME	STATUS
Mongolia, Asia	Extinct in the wild
DIET	YOUNG
Grass	One foal is born at a time

Przewalski's horse

Saved from extinction

The Przewalski (often pronounced Shev-al-skee) is the only undomesticated species of horse in the world.

These wild horses, from Mongolia and China in Asia, are named after an explorer called Colonel Przewalski, who discovered them in 1878.

The horses became very unpopular with the local Mongolian tribes, because they competed with their domestic cattle for grazing and water. As Przewalski's horses cannot be tamed and were therefore considered to be of no real use, the tribesmen shot them to protect their cattle's source of food.

During the last ten years, Przewalski's horses have almost certainly become extinct in the wild and it is only the success of international breeding programmes in zoos and wildlife parks that has kept the species alive.

So many horses have been bred in captivity that it has now become possible to return a herd back into the wild. Several zoos, including Marwell Zoo in Britain, have agreed with the Mongolian government to reintroduce the first herd of captive-bred Przewalski's horses back on to the Mongolian steppes, where they will live in a protected reserve. They will then be studied for a year or so to ensure that the horses can adapt to the extreme winter cold and high summer heat. If they do, they will then be moved to a much larger area in the Gobi Desert, which should provide the horses with a suitable habitat, back in the land of their ancestors.

Here's a horse you'll never be able to ride!

HOME	STATUS
Africa – from the Cape to Somalia	3,400 left in the world
DIET	**YOUNG**
Plants	A single calf is born at a time

Black rhinoceros

The mammal whose horn is worth more than its weight in gold

The rhino's massive body, thick skin and dramatic horns make it one of the most impressive animals in the world. They can measure over 3.5 m long, 1.8 m high at the shoulder and weigh over 2 tonnes. On average, their horn may be 0.6 m long, although 50 years ago, much longer horns were found, the record being 1.4 m.

The rhino lives a solitary life and does not move about much. It lives on the open savanna and rain forest of central, southern and eastern Africa and feeds on thorny or leathery plants, which it draws into its mouth with its mobile upper lip.

Rhinos have very poor vision and are unable to detect a motionless person at a distance of more than 30 m. Their eyes are placed on either side of their head so that in order to see straight ahead they peer first with one

eye and then with the other. They rely most on their sense of smell – the size of their nose system is larger than their brain!

Rhinos are not very intelligent, but this makes them dangerous and unpredictable. They have often been known to attack men or their vehicles.

IN DANGER!

Once, hundreds of thousands of rhinos roamed freely on the plains of Africa. Today they survive in small pockets in ten different countries including Zimbabwe, South Africa, Kenya and Tanzania. In the 1960s there was an estimated population of 65,000 black rhinos left in the wild, but now there are less than 3,400. In Kenya there are now less than 400.

Rhinos are shot (or even electrocuted) for their valuable horns. A rhino poacher in Africa can make more money by selling just one horn to a trader than he can from farming for a whole year.

A rhino horn is worth more per kilo than gold and powdered down by people in the Far East for medicinal purposes. It is also used to make special dagger handles worn by men in the Yemen as a status symbol.

Although some countries have now stopped importing rhino horn, China, South Korea, Taiwan and Thailand have not and, unless these markets are closed, the black rhino could become extinct in the wild by the year 2000.

A rhino's horn is not made of ivory like elephants' tusks, but of thick layers of keratin fibres, the same substance that our hair and fingernails are made of.

HOME
North Atlantic,
North Sea, Baltic
Sea, Arctic Ocean,
North Pacific

STATUS
The Juan Fernandez
and Monk seals are
threatened with
extinction

DIET
Fish

YOUNG
A single pup is born
at a time

Seal

The wide-eyed diver with sensitive whiskers

Seals have a very good sense of hearing and make a 'clicking' sound underwater. This is thought to act like an underwater radar and helps them find food, even in dark muddy estuaries. A seal's whiskers, which are very sensitive, also help them find food by detecting vibrations caused by fish as they swim through the water. Seals also have very

usually only dive below water for a few minutes, they can stay underwater a lot longer. When they sleep, which they usually do in shallow water, they automatically come up to breathe. When underwater they can make themselves completely watertight by closing their ears and nostrils.

Seals have a layer of fatty tissue, or blubber, under their skin, which can be more than 10 cm thick. This acts as insulation and prevents their bodies from losing too much heat in cold water.

good eyesight and can see clearly both above and below water. This is due to the way the backs of their eyes are designed to trap and reflect all the available light.

The Harbour, or Common, seal varies in length from 132 to 171 cm and, like many seals, is a very slow breather. Although seals

IN DANGER!

Seals have suffered badly at the hands of Man. They have been hunted for years, both for their warm, waterproof fur and for their oily fat layer. They are also killed by fishermen who think the seals could put them out of business by eating too many fish. Seals also die as a result of oil and chemical pollution in the water and often get caught up in plastic bags and other rubbish, which is tipped out of boats or left on the shore by careless members of the public.

Large numbers of Harp seals are killed every spring in Canada, and in Britain licences are still given to kill Grey seals. Although the Harbour, or Common, seal is not yet endangered, several other species, such as the Monk and the Juan Fernandez seal, are on the verge of extinction.

Fairy tern

The bird that lays its eggs on branches

Although more correctly named the White tern, this beautiful bird is popularly known as the Fairy tern in the tropical islands which it inhabits. It has snow-white plumage, with a dark bill and eye rings.

It does not make a nest but lays its single egg precariously balanced on the branch of a tree. Here, it becomes easy pickings for the skink, or lizard, which climbs up the tree and knocks the egg off its branch while the parents are away looking for fish. The skink then returns to the ground to eat the contents of the broken egg.

Unlike most sea-birds, which have webbed feet, the Fairy tern has hooked feet which enable it to stand on branches without falling off. The young chick will stand in its tree while its parents catch and feed it with fresh fish. While many other adult birds will swallow food and then regurgitate it (cough it up) into the mouths of their young, the Fairy tern brings whole, small fish for its chicks to eat.

HOME	STATUS
Asia	Endangered
DIET	**YOUNG**
Ox, wild boar, deer, peacock, fish	Two or three cubs are born every one or two years

Tiger

The world's best-dressed man-eater!

The tiger, with its magnificent coat, is one of the most beautiful members of the cat family, but is also thought of as a man-eater. In fact, most tigers prefer to stay away from people and it is only sick and wounded animals, which cannot hunt their usual prey, that cause the forty or so deaths each year in India.

The tiger is an excellent swimmer and, in times of flood, has been known to swim from one island to another in search of food. Unlike most members of the cat family it is not a very good climber and does not usually climb trees.

The tiger's prey is mainly deer, wild pig and smaller animals such as monkeys and even porcupines, but it will also catch fish and turtles in times of flood as well as locusts in a swarm. Tigers do not appear to be able to see stationary animals very easily, even at close range, but their hearing is extremely good and this is the sense they use most when stalking their prey.

Tigers usually give birth to 2 or 3 cubs at a time, although occasionally, there can be as many as 7. They are born blind and helpless, but their coats have their parents' striped pattern.

When they are 7 months old, they can kill for themselves, but usually stay with their mother until they are 2 years old during which time she teaches them more advanced hunting skills.

When a tiger cub is born, it weighs less than half as much as a human baby.

IN DANGER!
The tiger has been hunted by Man for many years for its coloured, striped coat. There were about 100,000 tigers living in Asia in 1900, but by 1972 there were only 5,000. This severe decline in numbers has led to the creation of one of the largest conservation projects ever known.

'Operation Tiger', launched by the World Wide Fund for Nature and the Indian Government, has set up special reserves in India, Bangladesh and Nepal and, as a result of these efforts, there are now thought to be approximately 7,000 tigers living in the wild.

HOME	STATUS
Galapagos Islands, Aldabra	Exact numbers not known
DIET	**YOUNG**
Grass, leaves and fruit	Up to 20 eggs are laid a year

Giant tortoise

The 200 year old animals threatened by the Greenhouse Effect

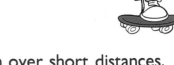

These people are weighing Esmerelda - the largest Giant tortoise in the world!

Giant tortoises grow up to 1.5 m long and can weigh more than 200 kg. They live longer than any other animal in the world, possibly up to 200 years! In the same way that a tree can be aged by counting the annular rings in its trunk, the age of a tortoise can be established by the ring markings on its shell, or carapace.

Although tortoises have the reputation of being very slow-moving animals, they can walk as fast as a man over short distances.

Giant tortoises were once so common in the Galapagos Islands off the coast of Ecuador, that early explorers claimed it was possible to walk long distances on the tortoises' shells without touching the ground. However, over the years, pirates and whalers reduced their numbers by taking hundreds of thousands of live tortoises on to their ships as a source of fresh meat.

One of the projects being undertaken to safeguard the species is 'Operation Curieuse'. Several hundred Aldabran tortoises have been transferred to one of the higher, inner islands of the Seychelles called Curieuse, in order to establish a stand-by colony should disaster overtake Aldabra. Special nurseries have been built on Curieuse where newly-born tortoises will live, safe from predators, until they are older and more independent.

HOME	STATUS
Tropical and temperate forests	Exact numbers not known
DIET	**YOUNG**
Insects	Many eggs are laid, which turn into tadpoles and then into frogs

Tree frog

The amphibian with sticky feet

Tree frogs live in tropical and temperate parts of the world and, as you can guess from their name, are specially adapted to living in trees. Their sticky toe pads help them cling upside down under leaves, which protect them from the hot sun and predators such as snakes and birds.

Their large, bulging eyes give them a wide-angle view of their surroundings and binocular vision, which helps them to gauge distances when ambushing passing insects. They are excellent jumpers and can launch themselves several metres in order to catch their unsuspecting prey.

The Seychelles Tree frog, from the Indian Ocean, is unique and has no close relatives among other living frogs. Its ancestors probably came to the Seychelles Islands from Africa or Madagascar several million years ago. The female is green in colour and much larger than the male, which is either light or dark brown.

Tree frogs sing and, on rainy nights, choruses of them can often be heard. The singing is thought to establish ownership of territories and also to attract females.